LIGHTNING BOLT BOOKS™

Hero Service Dogs

Jennifer Boothroyd

Lerner Publications • Minneapolis

For Laurel

Lerner Publications Company
A division of Lerner Publishing Group, Inc.
241 First Avenue North
Minneapolis, MN 55401 USA

For reading levels and more information, look up this title at www.lernerbooks.com.

Library of Congress Cataloging-in-Publication Data

Names: Boothroyd, Jennifer, 1972- author.
Title: Hero service dogs / Jennifer Boothroyd.
Description: Minneapolis : Lerner Publications, 2017. | Series: Lightning bolt books : hero dogs | Includes bibliographical references and index.
Identifiers: LCCN 2016012836 (print) | LCCN 2016027067 (ebook) | ISBN 9781512425413 (lb : alk. paper) | ISBN 9781512431100 (pb : alk. paper) | ISBN 9781512428025 (eb pdf)
Subjects: LCSH: Service dogs—Juvenile literature.
Classification: LCC HV1569.6 .B66 2017 (print) | LCC HV1569.6 (ebook) | DDC 362.4/048—dc23

LC record available at https://lccn.loc.gov/2016012836

Manufactured in the United States of America
1-41309-23253-5/18/2016

Table of Contents

Guide Dogs

Why is this dog in a grocery store? It is a service dog! Service dogs are working dogs trained to help their owners.

Guide dogs help people who are blind or who can't see well. These dogs lead people around.

Guide dogs make sure their owners don't fall or walk into something.

Guide dogs wear a special harness. The dog's owner holds on to the harness when walking.

When an owner says "steady," he or she wants the dog to slow down.

Guide dogs listen for commands from their owners. They learn commands such as *left, right,* and *forward.*

A guide dog will stop at curbs and steps. This warns the owner that something is in the way.

Guide dogs make sure cars are stopped before crossing the street.

Guide dogs sometimes need to disobey their owners. A guide dog will not follow a command that leads its owner into danger.

A guide dog won't let its owner be hit by a car.

Assistance Dogs

Someone who can't move easily might have an assistance dog. Assistance dogs help people who have trouble with some tasks.

Assistance dogs can help their owners open doors.

Assistance dogs can be asked to reach things for their owners. Some assistance dogs help their owners move around.

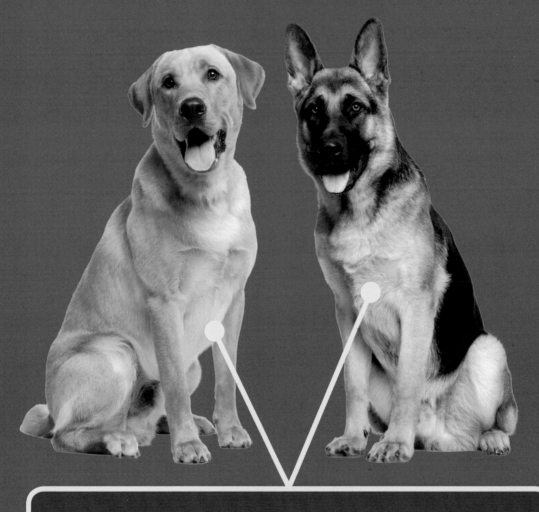

Labrador retrievers and German shepherds make good assistance dogs.

Assistance dogs can be trained to flip a light switch. They can also learn how to open automatic doors.

Many people with assistance dogs are in wheelchairs. Assistance dogs are trained to stay safe and calm around wheelchairs.

A big part of an assistance dog's job is to wait for commands. Assistance dogs are trained to wait out of the way until their owners ask for help.

A service dog is always ready, even when it is resting.

Service dogs have an important job. They are always there to keep their owners safe!

Service dogs often wear vests when they are working. Never pet a service dog without the owner's permission.

Hearing Dogs

Hearing dogs help people who are deaf or who have trouble hearing. These dogs are trained to listen for important sounds.

This hearing dog heard the alarm clock!

Many types of dogs
can be trained to work
as hearing dogs.

Some dogs are adopted
from animal shelters and
trained to be hearing dogs.

When a hearing dog hears something important, it will get its owner's attention. Then it leads the owner to the sound.

This dog tells its owner when the oven timer rings.

Hearing dogs might lie down or nudge their owners if they hear a fire alarm.

It might not be safe to move toward a sounding fire alarm.

All hearing dogs learn different sounds. A dog must know at least three sounds to become a hearing dog. They are trained to respond to these sounds within fifteen seconds!

Like all service dogs, hearing dogs are allowed in places pet dogs aren't.

Medical Response Dogs

Medical response dogs are trained to help people with special medical conditions. Some people with diabetes or epilepsy have medical response dogs.

Medical devices help some diabetics manage their condition.

Dogs have a much stronger sense of smell than people. Many scientists believe this lets dogs sense certain sudden medical changes.

A medical response dog might sense when its owner is about to have a medical emergency.

Some people with severe allergies depend on medical response dogs. The dogs alert their owners if an allergen is nearby.

Peanuts are a common allergen.

Medical response dogs can often sense a problem before their owners know something is wrong. The dog may encourage its owner to lie down or to take a special medicine.

Some people with certain conditions may need to lie down or take certain medications if there is a medical emergency.

Medical response dogs react when their owner's symptoms get worse. They can get help from nearby people if needed.

Some medical response dogs will bring their owners medicine.

Medical response dogs and other service dogs get plenty of time to play, just like regular pets. Playing together helps make service dogs and their owners better friends and partners.

Service dogs and their owners depend on each other!

History of Service Dogs

Did you know that a German doctor named Gerhard Stalling opened the first guide dog training school in 1916? It's true! Here are some fascinating facts about the school.

- Stalling's school trained dogs to help soldiers that became blind during World War I (1914-1918).

- The school grew, and eventually, the dogs were sent to help blind people in countries all around the world.

- The school closed in the 1920s. But Stalling's idea had spread. Another large school near the city of Berlin was also training dogs.

Top Dog

Tatiana is a trained hearing and medical response dog. She lives with her owner, Cristina Saint-Blancard, in Plantation, Florida. One night when Cristina was having trouble breathing, Tatiana woke up Cristina's parents. Her parents called an ambulance. Tatiana saved Cristina's life! Tatiana was nominated for an American Humane Association Hero Dog Award. She is truly a top dog!

Glossary

allergen: a substance that causes an allergic reaction

blind: little or no eyesight

command: a direction to do something

deaf: little or no hearing

diabetes: a disease where there is too much sugar in the blood

disobey: to not follow directions

epilepsy: a disease that causes abnormal electrical activity in the brain. Epilepsy can make someone pass out or have seizures, where muscles may twitch.

harness: straps worn by an animal to help a human control it

symptom: a sign related to a medical condition

Further Reading

Canines for Kids: Types of
Service Dogs
http://caninesforkids.org/service-dogs

Fishman, Jon M. *Hero Therapy Dogs.* Minneapolis:
Lerner Publications, 2017.

Hoffman, Mary Ann. *Helping Dogs.* New York:
Gareth Stevens, 2011.

How Guide Dogs Work
http://animals.howstuffworks.com/animal-facts
/guide-dog1.htm

Montalván, Luis Carlos. *Tuesday Tucks Me In: The
Loyal Bond between a Soldier and His Service Dog.*
New York: Roaring Brook, 2014.

Index

Photo Acknowledgments

The images in this book are used with the permission of: © iStockphoto.com/Luis Alvarez, p. 2; © De Meester Johan/Arterra Picture Library/Alamy, p. 4; © Colin McConnell/Toronto Star/Getty Images, p. 5; © iStockphoto.com/HultonArchive, p. 6; © iStockphoto.com/ Cylonphoto, p. 7; © Westend61/SuperStock, p. 8; © Jeroen van den Broek/Shutterstock.com, p. 9; AP Photo/Patrick Record/The Ann Arbor News, p. 10; © Eric Isselee/Shutterstock.com, p. 11 (Labrador retriever); © iStockphoto.com/GlobalP, pp. 11 (German shepherd), 17; Hans Gutknecht/ZUMAPRESS/Newscom, p. 12; © Tommy Maenhout/Dreamstime.com, p. 13; © F1 ONLINE/SuperStock, p. 14; © Susan Schmitz/Shutterstock.com, p. 15; © iStockphoto.com/ Chris Pecoraro, p. 16; © Graham Franks/Alamy, p. 18; © iStockphoto.com/Chimpinski, p. 19; Jonathan Banks/REX/Newscom, p. 20; © ZUMA Press/Alamy, p. 21; © iStockphoto.com/ Imagesbybarbara, p. 22; © Marsia16/Dreamstime.com, p. 23; © iStockphoto.com/Alasdair Thomson, p. 24; © iStockphoto.com/PJPhoto69, p. 25; © iStockphoto.com/PK-Photos, p. 26; © Hyoung Chang/Denver Post/Getty Images, p. 27; © iStockphoto.com/Mark Kostich, p. 31.

Front cover: © Boris Djuranovic/Dreamstime.com.

Main body text set in Billy Infant regular 28/36. Typeface provided by SparkType.